Affiliate Marketing

Joining Top Affiliate Networks And Programs, Managing Ads, And Generating Traffic: The Complete Guide

(The Comprehensive Step-by-step Guide To Going From Novice To Top Affiliate)

Luciano Cherubini

TABLE OF CONTENT

Introduction 1

Chapter 1: Developing Your Content Planning Calendars 11

Chapter 2: Developing A Clientele And Selling Products 18

Chapter 3: Automatic Seo Methodology 34

Chapter 4: Profitable Affiliate Marketing Techniques Employed By Google 44

Chapter 5: Promote Your Blog 52

Chapter 6: Artificial Intelligence 61

Chapter 7: Tracking And Optimization 84

Chapter 8: Various Methods For Selling Physical Goods 93

Chapter 9: How To Address The Drop Shipping Issue 114

Introduction

Due to the advancing age of technology and the ease that comes with it, an increasing number of people are looking for methods to use technology as a source of income and also work remotely from home. Affiliate marketing is one industry that enables this, and it has grown substantially over the past few years. It has grown so substantially that for many individuals, it is now their primary source of income, as opposed to their secondary source.

Affiliate marketing's widespread accessibility is one of the primary factors contributing to its popularity. You need no prior experience to become an affiliate marketer, and you can get started for almost nothing.

Starting a new job is unquestionably a risky opportunity; you will either flourish or fail. In the new era of modern technology, you should never underestimate your power if you choose Affiliate Marketing as a career. The internet affiliate marketing industry is estimated to be worth $1 billion and is anticipated to grow in the coming years. This exhaustive guide to the affiliate marketing industry will teach you every aspect of the industry.

Phone Advertising

Many individuals worry about telephone marketing, and with good reason. In many situations, you are speaking with someone you do not recognize and cannot discern over the phone. The added disadvantage is that you cannot see their face. In phone marketing, however, if you pay close attention to how people react to you and listen to what they say and how they say it, you can become quite adept at assessing a prospect or client over the phone.

Fear of the unknown on the other end of the line, fear of what they may say or do, is the most difficult to overcome. The majority of people are willing to speak with you, particularly if they requested a phone call in the first place. Therefore, all you need to do is converse!

This is easier than you may believe. Try the following in a conversational manner, rather than as a sales proposal. Substitute terms that you believe work better with your personality and writing style.

Hi (name) (name). I'm (your name) calling from (your city). (Name), this is just a brief courtesy call, but you visited my website and submitted a form requesting information on developing a home-based income.

Do you remember doing it?

(Wait for a response even if there is a one-minute pause) Excellent!

I just wanted to briefly introduce myself over the phone. And to tell you a little bit about our (product/service/opportunity) and why this opportunity would be appealing to you, given that it has no competitors in the network marketing industry, which is VERY rare and uncommon.

How committed are you to establishing a home-based income?

The response will reveal a great deal about the person with whom you are speaking. Whether they query whether this is an MLM scam or not, you immediately know you do not want to do business with this person. If they say, "Well, sort of, but how hard do I have to work?" you would respond as follows:

"You know, I don't believe you're a good fit for this opportunity. "We appreciate your time."

Then you TRANSITION! You cannot force someone to be interested in or desire labor; they either are or are not.

IF you receive a response such as "I'm extremely serious" or words to that effect, proceed to the second stage of your phone conversation and say:

Perfect! Do you have approximately five minutes for me to explain our (product/service/opportunity)?

WAIT FOR ANSWER. If they respond YES, continue to the next step.

"I am a member of (your organization/group/etc.)." And I have some fascinating information about s(group/business/product) to share with you. Are you prepared to hear what we have to say?

WAIT FOR THE RESPONSE!

If the answer is No, continue on. If so, please provide a brief description of your product/company/services, etc.

You must have all of this written down, similar to a screenplay, or you will become disoriented. When you're finished, ask:

Quite intriguing concept, right?

WAIT FOR THE RESPONSE

If the answer is no, proceed. If they respond positively, invite them to join your team/business/purchase your product.

Some aspects of this conversation may veer off course, but the nice thing is that you're conversing with a human who will have questions. As long as you know your products, business strategy, and staff, you can discuss your work with anyone.

Speak to the individual as if you were conversing with someone seated across the table from you during lunch or coffee. If your prospect is not interested in or does not want what you are offering, that is their choice. There is no point in arguing differently with them. If you do so, you will become one of those annoying Internet marketers who cannot comprehend the word NO.

Accept a refusal with decorum and courtesy. In the majority of cases, it is not a personal rejection. Leave things as they are and accept their choice as it is. Respecting their preferences will earn you significantly more points over time. You may revisit the offer at any time in the future. Sometimes, no means no, not at this time.

Do not attempt to persuade them into joining you by promising them unlimited income or that earning money or building a business with you is SO EASY. Why then? Because the actuality of the situation is that starting a business is laborious work. Be sincere and straightforward. Yes, it will require significant effort, but you will be there to help them succeed.

In response to someone offering you information about a business opportunity, you send a bounce back. You must respond to them on a personal level with a concise, to-the-point letter, as they are obviously actively promoting and you may be able to use them for your team/business. To receive opportunities such as these, submit your business email to a FREE auto responder testing site. Numerous websites sell email addresses, and you can quickly be added to hundreds of mailing lists.

An auto responder is a mail utility that sends a reply to an email message automatically. They provide information on a topic without requiring the requester to do anything more than provide an email address. In addition, they serve to convey affirmation that the communication was received. Depending on the severity of your email service provider's filters and the email provider you employ, the majority of bounced emails wind up in your bulk folder or spam filter box.

15. Improve your campaigns

As an affiliate marketer, it is essential to continually seek methods to optimize your campaigns. There are a number of factors that can affect your affiliate marketing performance, and by paying close attention to them, you can maximize the effectiveness of your efforts.

Consider the following factors as you optimize your affiliate marketing campaigns:
- Ensure that you're targeting the appropriate audience. Affiliate marketing is all about targeting the appropriate audience with the appropriate offer. If you do not target the appropriate audience, you will not see results.

- Keep your conversion rate in mind. This is the percentage of individuals who perform the desired action (such as making a purchase or subscribing to a newsletter) after clicking on your affiliate link. A low conversion rate indicates that either your offer or your target audience needs improvement.

- Test, test, test. Always evaluate various aspects of your affiliate marketing campaigns to determine what yields the best results. Try out various offers, advertisement copy, landing pages, etc. The only method to determine what works best is to conduct experiments.

By paying attention to these factors, you can maximize the effectiveness of your affiliate marketing campaigns.

Chapter 1: Developing Your Content Planning Calendars

Content calendars, also known as editorial calendars, are essential for social media development. They help you plan and organize your ideas so that they are cohesive and you have ample time to produce high-impact, results-driven content. Creating your content calendar is straightforward, but there are a few steps you'll need to take to ensure that it is targeted and effective.

The Calendar of Know, Like, Trust, and Sell
In the previous chapter, I enumerated three primary content types: likable, relationship-building, and sales content. In this chapter, we will further dissect the sales funnel using the following four words: know, like, trust, and sell.

Through the creation of appealing content, you generate "know" and "like." This indicates that individuals discover your page and decide they like you. This should correspond to two content elements in your content calendar.

Your relationship-building content establishes "trust" in your sales funnel, after which your sales content remains the same. Each of these two distinct categories should account for one position.

With this breakdown in mind, it is now possible to comprehend the structure of the "know, like, trust, sell content" calendar. In other words, you will construct a content calendar that alternates between these four content goals. Now, you simply need to determine how many times per week you intend to create content and start creating by alternating between these content foci. For instance, if you intend to post three times per week on Instagram, TikTok, or Facebook, you would alternately post three pieces of know, like, trust, and sell content per month.

If you are producing long-form video content, such as YouTube videos, you should strive to include all four of these components in each and every video. Know and like should occur within the first thirty seconds, trust should comprise the majority of the video, and selling should occur within the final thirty seconds. Because you can pack so much information into a single video, it is reasonable to produce no more than one or two per week.

Developing Market-Specific Content That Sells

Now that you grasp the structure of the know, like, trust, sell content calendar, we must discuss the significance of selling-oriented, targeted content. Numerous novices commit the grave error of producing aimless content to fulfill their content calendar's objectives. Although this will generate content for your feed, it will not generate revenues for your business. You must have a marketing-oriented content calendar. You may be surprised to discover that this begins with your very first item of 'know' content. Here are the five stages to creating targeted, sellable content:

What is your main objective?

What are you launching or attempting to sell at this time? Are you a brand-new company, or are you launching your tenth business? Do you offer a discount on something you're selling? Define your content's objective or the direction you're directing readers in the next 1 to 4 weeks.

What must individuals know?

What information must individuals possess for this objective to be achieved? What must they know about you and your business for them to like you? What information about the product or service do they need to be interested? What must they know about the promotion that will likely capture their attention?

What must individuals like?

What do individuals need to know to realize that they enjoy your product or service? What kind of content will make them like your brand as a whole and remain loyal? Why should they choose you over others in your niche? What can you do that is relatable and entertaining and attracts individuals to your brand and offer?

What must individuals have faith in?

How do consumers know that your brand is the best? How do they know you will take advantage of the promotion? How will they know if their purchase was satisfactory? Do you have social substantiation that demonstrates that others were satisfied with their purchases from you?

What must individuals purchase?

Specifically, what are you selling? What are the highlights of this sale that will captivate your audience the most? What should they know before purchasing this special offer? What specific actions are required for them to take advantage of the special offer?

Answers to these specific queries should be reflected in the content on your content calendar. You should find inventive ways to communicate with your audience, entertain or educate them, and provide them with the information they need to discover, like, and purchase your brand. In this manner, every piece of content is targeted and effective.

Chapter 2: Developing A Clientele And Selling Products

Promoting affiliate products to earn money requires establishing credibility and trust with your target audience. Herein lies the "catch" (if there is one), as maximization of profits requires genuine effort. The good news is that if you choose something you're truly passionate about, you can earn a lot of money while doing something you enjoy. This cannot occur, however, until you have established yourself as an authority figure and developed a following.

What other promotional channels exist for affiliate products? Clearly, absolutely! This chapter will also explore such subjects. Nonetheless, it is to your advantage to cultivate a following and ensure that consumers value your product. Making a Successful Brand: The Essence: Obtaining such influence is not a straightforward endeavor. Before people will purchase products simply because you promote them, you must put in a great deal of effort and provide genuine long-term value. The first steps in this regard are a website and active social media profiles. Instead of immediately attempting to make a transaction, focus on establishing rapport and brand loyalty by consistently releasing high-quality content. What is most important? Create a unique, memorable brand with a compelling vision and a well-defined target market. (In the consumer persona, the "perfect customer" is portrayed.) Most people make the fatal error of designing a website that covers too much ground in an attempt to satisfy everyone. Similar to the practice of purchasing digital products in the first place, this can be a poor strategy. The reason for this is that when a brand becomes extensive, it inevitably becomes monotonous and uninspiring.

For instance, a website devoted to "fitness" is monotonous and saturated with the same information. It is comparable to competing against the entire internet. How do you distinguish yourself in such a congested marketplace? Consider instead launching a website dedicated to fitness for individuals over 40. The alternative is Paleo Fitness. Alternatively, CrossFit. Physical activity outdoors. Or Extreme Muscle Development. Each of these alternatives has a more distinct clientele, a more compelling raison d'être, and an intriguing premise. They will each have a reduced target audience, but those they do reach will be MUCH more invested in and enthusiastic about discovering something tailored to their specific interests. The inception of the brand should be motivated by this solitary, compelling purpose. The design of your logo and website must be instantaneously recognizable and appealing to your target audience. You must make it obvious to your target audience and topic that your brand is for them, and then support that claim with content. The color scheme of the extreme bodybuilding website will be red and black, and it will feature numerous somber images of extremely muscular men as well as articles titled "raising testosterone with compound lifts."

In contrast, a paleo fitness website will likely be designed in green and white, with images of individuals running in natural environments. From now on, EVERYTHING, including advertisements and social media postings, must adhere to this image. It is essential to choose an affiliate product that effectively communicates with the intended audience. And you will promote and sell the product to consumers in this manner. Additionally, you must present new information that demonstrates your actual competence. Here's a shocker: you will never advertise the affiliate product if you hire a writer who lacks subject expertise. Why? A contracted author is limited to researching the topic and restating the information in their own words. It also means that they probably won't be able to determine if the information is out-of-date or inaccurate, since they won't know the subject well enough to recognize when either of those conditions apply. Either compose it yourself or hire a writer who is extremely passionate about the subject. Why? Consequently, they have something new and interesting to contribute to the discussion. People will follow your lead, heed your counsel, and join your cause if you provide them with something novel to consider.

Do something daring. Think creatively outside the frame. Exhibit enthusiasm for your work. Choose a product that targets the same demographic. Cannot afford the time? There are additional options available in addition to those listed. Linking Your Site Within the affiliate marketing industry, sales are simple. You are given a single link to promote a product and can earn commissions regardless of where you post it online. The only dilemma remaining is where to place it.

While the majority of us will direct traffic to a dedicated sales page, there are other options. This section will investigate this mechanism in addition to several others. Making a Marketing Page A merchant website is a website whose principal objective is to generate sales. In other terms, it will not provide additional information, such as links or advertisements. You must eliminate anything that could cause customers to lose interest in your service or product.

Typically, the architecture of a sales page will be long and narrow, requiring visitors to scroll down the page and spend more time with your content. Customers will have a much more difficult time exiting the store without making a purchase. However, the writing is the most important aspect. A persuasive sales proposal can convert this attentive audience into eager customers. You will become a marketing master if you conquer the art of persuasion through writing. If you came to see drones, you've come to the incorrect place... Ultimately, you will be much more successful at making sales, getting people to sign up for your list, and achieving your goals if you know how to manipulate words to persuade an audience. Therefore, how does one master this extraordinary ability? The following recommendations should prove beneficial... People are usually pressed for time and disinterested in perusing lengthy passages. Therefore, it is essential to rapidly gain their attention. Getting them to comprehend what you have to say is the first step in convincing them to accept your viewpoint. How does the process work? Effective strategies commence with assertive statements.

One more is to have people read a story to pique their interest. It is usually very difficult to dissuade people from reading to the conclusion of such a story! To cite numerical evidence: Given that they haven't met you and already know you're attempting to sell them something, not everyone will automatically believe what you say. Instead, you should allow the data to speak for themselves. Your argument will carry more weight if you include pertinent data and cite pertinent authorities. Anticipate your audience's concerns and address them head-on. You can use phrases such as "there are a plethora of fantastic-sounding online offerings," but emphasize that this is not "just another scam." Reduce risk: "loss aversion" is an inborn human characteristic. Therefore, they are more concerned with maintaining their current possessions than with expanding their horizons through the acquisition of something new. You should eliminate any risk by providing money-back guarantees and complimentary trials. Know first and foremost what you are selling. Emotional value is the promise that your product will enhance your customers' lives. You should specify that the eBook you're selling on fitness is not about fitness. Your true product is the sensation of boundless energy, rock-hard midsection, and unshakeable confidence. You must pay careful consideration to that! Utilize emotive language to elicit a favorable response from the reader, preferably the desire to buy your product.

Keep in mind that many informational products already have sales pages, such as this one, from which you can copy and paste the text verbatim into your website. Now that you've established a sales page, all you need to do to begin generating conversions is refer people to it. Emails and social media posts regarding the product are two effective methods for achieving this goal. Place product advertisements in the website's right-hand column and other pertinent locations. Establishing Shop If you intend to sell multiple affiliate products (another excellent strategy), you should establish a shop. In other words, as you would in an online store, you will highlight and promote specific products that align with your brand's ethos. The only perceptible change is that buyers will now be redirected to external pages when they click on your product. This is easy; for example, the WooCommerce e-commerce plugin for WordPress can assist you in getting begun. Therefore, visitors can purchase directly from your website. Users can select an item to be redirected to a new page containing their affiliate link.

What about adding in-text links to your content, though? Although it is an excellent method for making money, few affiliates employ it. Simply write about topics you're interested in and embed an affiliate link to earn money as a blogger. This method of subtle product promotion increases the likelihood that interested readers will click on the link. Similar to incorporating AdSense into your website, except you receive a larger share of the revenue and can actively encourage your readers to select the link. You can even acknowledge that it is financially beneficial. Many jurisdictions mandate financial disclosure for the sale of such items. Using a plugin that appends a message to the bottom of each page on your website is a straightforward method for achieving this objective; just don't neglect to do it! Writing a top ten list is an effective method for promoting affiliate products. In the fitness industry, you could assemble a list of the top five pieces of home gym equipment, whereas a tech writer could compile a list of the market's top five most efficient laptops.

In either case, you will be able to generate clicks and revenue due to the natural match between your content and rich snippets, which will help your content stand out in the SERPs. As a result, there is no reason why you cannot include a referral link in an email's body. This is an excellent method for delivering your message directly to the inboxes of potential consumers when they are most likely to respond to the offers you're sending. eBooks are another medium where affiliate links can be incorporated. You can embed hyperlinks in a PDF if you sell or distribute a digital product. People who read this are likely invested in your brand and will heed your advice. With these highly qualified leads, you can attempt to close a transaction for a more expensive product with confidence. Consider the following scenario: you sell a multimedia project for $20, a ton of people read it, and you make a ton more money because they followed your advice. Consider printing a brochure with your affiliate link. Creating a brief and straightforward URL that ultimately leads to your affiliate program is the best way to take advantage of this. Thus, you can directly promote your products to potential customers. The recommendations above are intended to demonstrate that you can experiment with a gentler sales approach by simply adding a link (possibly accompanied by an image) to the product.

This works exceptionally well for tangible objects. This method of incorporating buy links can result in numerous minor sales, which, when added together, can amount to a significant sum if you have a successful website with many visitors and a variety of content. You must be inventive in conceiving of additional affiliate link applications. You never know which strategy will yield the best results for your products until you experiment with a variety of approaches. Methods of Advertising Suppose that, aside from Pay-Per-Click, nobody is there to attend to you. What if you are unable to persuade your audience as a credible authority figure? Consequently, you must devise strategies to direct traffic directly to your sales page. The good news is that Pay-Per-Click (PPC) platforms such as Facebook and AdWords make this exceedingly straightforward. Pay-per-click (PPC) advertising only necessitates payment when a user clicks on the advertisement. Setting an utmost "per click" spend and a budget cap is solely your responsibility. If your cost per click is too low, your ad will not appear if there is a lot of advertising from competing firms within the same category. If you set the price too high, you will incur a financial loss.

Facebook advertising enables you to target users based on the information they have made public. Age, gender, location, interests, profession, income, and the preferences of others are all important considerations. Certainly, there is more! AdWords advertising on Google is designed to take into account the person's interests (based on how they're searching for "keywords") and their intent. One of the most important aspects of pay-per-click advertising is determining the user's intent, which can disclose whether they are merely browsing or considering a purchase. Google search results for "greatest computer games of the year" They may search for the game by name or for "cheap computer games" if they are in the market to purchase. Negative keywords can eliminate search queries with inappropriate intent (such as "free download") because they indicate that the user is not interested in making a purchase.

The objective of pay-per-click marketing is to attract only serious prospective consumers to your website. This reduces expenses while increasing potential earnings. This implies that the ads must be "targeted" as precisely as possible, to the point where they may frighten away those who aren't likely to make a purchase if they're phrased incorrectly. The link should direct readers directly to a sales page for maximum profit. Next, you should prioritize the conversion rate of your website. In other words, if your homepage is well-written, you may see a 1% conversion rate (meaning that 1% of site visitors make a purchase). A higher ROI allows for increased marketing spending without sacrificing profits. Directly Selling to Customers Using Social Media and Other Channels You may also choose to sell your products directly via these channels. You can readily promote affiliate programs on

Instagram and Facebook. If you do not have the knowledge or opportunity to create a website, this is an excellent alternative for reaching your target audience.

Chapter 3: Automatic Seo Methodology

To rank on search engines, you must comprehend how SEO works, as it is the only way to generate sales, traffic, and leads for your company. If you want to make money through affiliate marketing, you don't have to wait around. This is a viable method for generating income.

The benefits of website optimization guarantee the success of your business, but only if your website ranks on the first page of Google search results, as 98% of Google users only view the first page of search results, whereas 40% of Google users click on sponsored ads.

Assuming you optimize your site to rank organically in the search bar, you will almost certainly observe positive results. However, you are by no means the only one struggling to make this happen. Since SEO provides so many opportunities for businesses, every business owner has optimized their content for higher rankings.

To rank higher on the first page, your website must adhere to Google's teams and conditions. However, despite the fact that many websites struggle to appear on the first page of a Google search, this does not mean that you should give up.

Simply invest more time, energy, money, and effort into your business to outsmart your competitors. Then you'll succeed!

However, you will need to understand how search engine optimization works, the appropriate keywords to use, and how to create high-quality web content.

Five Done For You SEO Methodologies

Step 1: Analyze the performance of your competitors

Analyzing your competitors' performance is an excellent technique for website optimization. Learn about;

The equipment they are using
How are they coping with the situation?
How much are their expenditures?
What are they failing to do?
Why do individuals like them?
Understand their distinct selling proposition
How can your business resemble theirs?
These are a few factors to keep in mind when attempting to determine what your competitors are doing well and how you can effectively imitate their strategies. You can only replicate a business strategy with a high SEO score, and you should never conduct business research without a plan.
I am confident in saying this because I was able to achieve success in this online business by emulating other people's

successful business strategies, tactics, and procedures. But prior to this, I wasted three years formulating unsuccessful business proposals.

Step 2: Spread Like Wildfire On Social Media

You may question how social media relates to search engine optimization. That is an excellent topic. Social media are platforms where you connect, interact, and transact with your consumers, whereas SEO helps to optimize and viralize your business.

Social media does not influence or guarantee how search engine optimization determines which websites to rank highly and which to rank low.

This is how it functions!

SEO attempts to rank your website based on its data and performance, and the algorithm uses this information to determine your website's level and placement when people search for keywords related to your business.

One of the factors considered by the algorithm is how people interact with your social media page, which may include;

Using targeted keywords
Your AdWords ad campaign
The information you publish
The traffic that your social media profiles generate
In contrast, social media facilitates communication and interaction with your consumers. You can become ubiquitous on social media if;

Utilize popular hashtags.
Have many followers.
Your social media pages generate traffic from the content you publish.

It is extremely difficult to grow your social media pages, but following the steps outlined in the preceding sections will make it simpler for you to achieve your goals, as going viral on social media increases your sales revenue.

Increasing your social media followers is free. You only need to publish high-quality content that assists people in solving their problems. Most blog posts and articles will advise you to purchase social media followers if you want to grow quickly on the Internet, but there are drawbacks to this strategy.

The disadvantages of purchasing social media followers can have positive or negative effects on your business, depending on your business objectives.

How I Do It (Excerpt)

When I entered affiliate marketing, it was no longer common practice to spam your link to everyone (which is a good thing, as that is a terrible method to promote offers). Therefore, I began by publishing articles and evaluations about the products I was promoting.

Writing product evaluations is still an effective technique for promoting affiliate offers, but you can't just write about the products. While it should be one of the first things you do to gain a better comprehension of your product, reviews are not always what people seek.

If people are browsing for a product review, they are in the purchase phase of their buyer's journey, and those are hot leads for you. However, "product + review" are extremely competitive keywords to rank for. Everyone desires to hold this position.

In addition to composing reviews, you should target individuals who are attempting to identify their problems and find solutions for them. You wish to transition from writing reviews of everything to writing and answering queries that people have in the early stages of the buyer's journey. We are creating a path for individuals, regardless of where they are in their journey, that leads to our affiliate offer.

When I first began promoting affiliate offers, I began with Funnelytics and wrote a review about it. As I learned more about SEO and organic strategies, I made sure to begin answering these questions. This is how I began.

It takes time to build a large following on social media, and I am aware that many platforms are pay-to-play, or are becoming increasingly pay-to-play, over time. The longer a platform exists, the more it costs to reach individuals. I did not have a lot of money when I first began my career. I spent my last $600 on a lifetime subscription to Funnelytics, so I was essentially broke, which led me to pursue organic traffic.

Due to these circumstances, I became an SEO specialist. Because of this, a significant portion of what I do to promote affiliate offers revolves around organic marketing. Writing excellent content and awaiting Google's ranking. I've mentioned previously that SEO requires some effort, so it's a bit of a marathon. Occasionally, you can rank instantaneously and obtain a quick win, but most of the time you must wait 3, 6, or even a full year to rank. Sometimes it is necessary to contribute additional content.

And while it may eventually rank on page 1, it does not necessarily receive a large number of views. Only the best three to five results receive significant traffic, so you must employ other strategies.

I now promote my content on social media using MissingLettr, which allows me to schedule social media postings for an article for the next two weeks to one year, saving me time and allowing me to continually promote my content.

I'll go into greater depth about my current content marketing strategy and how I disseminate my content in a later chapter, but I wanted to give you a brief overview of how I operate in this chapter, since we're discussing marketing and content.

A Specific Overview Of Affiliate Marketing

You may be pondering how to earn money through affiliate marketing.

Don't fret, we are here to assist you. We have compiled a list of 100 tactics, tricks, and strategies for successful affiliate marketing. Therefore, whether you're a novice or a seasoned pro, you'll find something beneficial in this guide.

Affiliate marketing can be an excellent means to earn extra money, but it is not as simple as it may appear. There is a great deal of competition in the marketplace, and if you're not vigilant, it's easy to fall behind.

Therefore, it is essential to keep up with the most recent trends and techniques. Here is where we come in. We will show you everything you need to know about affiliate marketing to make money.

Chapter 4: Profitable Affiliate Marketing Techniques Employed By Google

An expert, Author Deon Christie, stated in one of his articles: "Now that you have seen the Keyword Research Tool, we can discuss the significance and role of keywords in relation to your level of achievement." Choosing a niche is also essential, so that you know which direction to pursue. Direction is significantly more essential than velocity, as 97% of affiliate marketers are moving in the wrong direction. The only distinction is that the 3% built their online empire on a foundation of keywords. You are searching for niche-specific keywords with a high search volume and low competition.

There are three categories of Primary Keyword Research Steps;

Short-Tail Keywords - These are singular keywords and are also known as Primary Keywords. These are the keywords you wish to include in your domain name; however, you must be objective and specific. Let's use the Dieting Niche as an example. Then, the best short-tail keywords will be Health, Diet, and Weight. These three keywords are searched approximately 982,000 times per month on Google. Can you see where this keyword thing is going?

Long Tail Keywords - These are typically comprised of no more than three keywords. Within the example market we're using, lose weight, losing weight, lose weight quickly, and fast weight loss are all outstanding Long Tail Keywords. They are searched approximately 564,100 times per month on Google. However, you will need to research the keywords pertinent to your niche, which will produce distinct results. Long-Tail Keywords are utilized on your website and in the post titles. Combining long and short tail keywords is extremely effective.

Anchor Text - These are Longer Keyword Phrases and refer to the phrase that a user will enter into their browser to search for a particular topic. The type of inquiry someone would conduct when they are extremely likely to make a purchase. How to lose weight, how to lose weight quickly, and the desire to lose weight are excellent examples for this purpose. Anchor text must be present on the home page of your website, as the Google Spider adores it and it aids in ranking. Google searches for these anchor texts 852,300 times per month. Now we will combine the results of the three previous exams.

Yes, 2,398.400 searches per month across the three search categories on Google. You must now be aware of the potential of keyword research and why only 3 percent of online marketers make such obscene quantities of money. This article will simplify the fundamentals of SEO, including what to include in headers, titles, categories, tag lines, and single tags. Additionally, Google Search Console includes a Site Map.

Choosing the H1 Heading - Occasionally serves as a Post or Blog Page Title, but typically refers to the Blog, Site, or Video Title. The H1 Heading is where you should include, within 15 to 65 characters, the primary search phrases for which you want your website or video to rank in Google.

Because the H1 Heading will appear at the top of Google Search Results pages, it is essential to limit its length to no more than sixty characters. Make the H1 Heading both Readable and Memorable.

Identifying the H2 Heading - This is typically the title of the blog post, and once again, the desired Search Phrases and Keywords must be incorporated into this Heading. Combining this with a "Reason Why"-style suggestion creates a successful H2 Heading.

Identifying the H3 Header - Post Titles and Widget Descriptions within the Blog sidebar frequently comprise the H3 Header. The "Alt="Attribute typically appears as an H3 Header when the Text Widget is used to load HTML code.

A Blog post Title also appears as an H3 Header when you use an SEO Plugin such as "All in One SEO Tools" and your Blog Post Title appears after the slash (/) preceding the Primary Domain. Using an SEO plugin will enable you to submit individual site maps for each of your pages, posts, tags, and categories.

Identifying the H4 Header - This is similar to the Tagline for your Blog Title Tag or H1 header. A Logo image is frequently approved as an H4 header by plugins that can display a logo icon.

The Site Map Description - Your Blog Site Map is vitally important; to create it, merely install the "Google XML SiteMaps" plugin. This Plugin will submit an updated Blog Site Map to the Google Search Console whenever you make modifications, but it may take a while (Normally 2 - 3 Weeks) for the modifications to appear in Search Results.

Despite having the Google SiteMaps Plugin activated, it is essential to manually verify Site Map Acceptance from within the Google Search Console. There may be instances when Google encounters errors with your Blog Site Map, preventing it from locating your blog.

You must then test the site map using the tools provided by Google Search Console, correct any errors discovered through your Blog C-Panel, and re-test the Site Map. When the results contain no errors, you can delete the previous site map and submit the new one.

Accessing the Google Search Console requires a Google account, as is the case with all the Free Tools Google provides, and there are a lot of them. You simply need to search in the appropriate locations and take your time learning how to use the tools. Simple Search your browser (Chrome is recommended) for "Google Search Console" and simply follow the instructions after clicking the link on the search results page.

The Blog Site Map is what Search Engine Spiders use to Crawl your Blog in order to correctly categorize it and send you the appropriate visitors. This is why the presence of Keywords and Search Phrases throughout all of your Blog's content, specifically in the appropriate positions, is so crucial.

Chapter 5: Promote Your Blog

Do you believe that publishing your content on your social accounts will benefit you? Sadly, that strategy will not work. Unless you have millions of followers who hang on every word you say.

Social media is one of the best traffic sources if used properly; otherwise, it is a waste of time. Let's see…

- Select the social networks that are most suitable for your blog.

- Contribute to groups on social media to share your abilities.

Engage with people on these networks and establish connections.

- Establish your own social media group or channel on Facebook, YouTube, WhatsApp, Snapchat, etc...

- Don't sell products directly. First, provide some value, then try to sell.

Always maintain a keen awareness of your competitors.

– Create a social media content calendar.

- Encourage users to identify additional individuals who could benefit from the content.

Never, ever purchase followers or admirers.

- Post regularly and frequently.

Email:

Email may be aging, but it is by no means obsolete. Incorporate email opt-ins on your blog (using extensions) and other channels (such as Facebook) to collect email addresses. To increase conversion, offer an exceptional freebie or regular recommendations exclusively to subscribers.

Then convert your subscribers into supporters. spread trending topics with a compelling call to action and encourage readers to spread them. Once you have a sizable email list, you will receive a substantial quantity of traffic.

Share-and-share websites:

When you share the content of others, you earn credits that allow you to publish your own content, which is then shared by others. ViralContentBee is among the finest sites for reciprocal sharing.

Forums like Quora:

Without a doubt, Quora is the greatest traffic source for your blog. To develop on Quora and avoid being blacklisted from the site, however, you must adhere to certain procedures.

Ask sincere and useful questions.

Try to respond to popular and prevalent questions.

- pose questions about the topic that are trending at the time you pose them.

- Do not use foul or inappropriate language.

- Do not explicitly share your affiliate link.

- Do not provide excessive links when responding.

After providing value, share one or two blog links in your response.

- Establish your own Quora section and grow an audience there.

- If your profile has a respectable amount of authority, Quora offers you the opportunity to profit as well.

Guest post:

It is like treasure for every blogger and advertiser. Connect with influencers and other content providers and request that they embed your content with a link back to your website. You can accomplish this by exchanging money or articles for a link. However, you must work with those individuals whose niche is the same as yours, or the partnership will not succeed.

Observations on other blogs:

By leaving insightful comments on other blogs in your niche, you can increase your credibility. Blog proprietors and other frequent commentators will recognize your name and begin to pay attention to your opinions.

You may also include the URL of your website in your comment. If you attempt to harass, you will be prevented from leaving comments on numerous prominent websites.

Sites for social bookmarking:

You can sign up for popular social bookmarking sites such as Pinterest, Reddit, Flipboard, etc... You can publish your content, including photos and videos, and organize them with categories. Then, other users can add your posts to their own message boards and share them with their audiences. Thus, this will also help you acquire traffic.

Notifications via push:

It is unquestionably the best and simplest method for retaining consumers. Using SMS notifications, you may be able to easily increase your returning visitors. You could use

OneSignal, which is both popular and free, to send push notifications.

Optimization for Search Engines

SEO reigns supreme among almost all traffic sources. As a novice, you simply adhere to the SEO recommendations provided by your SEO plugin, such as Yoast, Rank Math, etc... Because SEO is such a vast subject, you will acquire it gradually and through experience.

Paid marketing:

It is a paid method of advertising your content, and I only recommend it if you are already generating revenue and want to scale up, or if you are prepared to incur a loss. Facebook Advertisements, Google Search Ads, YouTube Ads, Native/Push Ads, and TikTok/Quora/Snapchat Ads are some cost-effective and popular options.

There are numerous additional methods to market your blog. But I believe these tips are sufficient for you as a beginner to market your blog's content and generate income.

The subsequent stage is Earning Money... Excited?

Let's dive...

Your Every Purchase Matters To US!

We have not intentionally done anything wrong; if anything has upset you, we sincerely apologize and ask your forgiveness.

We provide this service at no cost whatsoever. We earn more money when you purchase more, and we hope you'll buy us a cup of coffee.

Happy Blogging, Happy Marketing...

Have a Healthy, Wealthy, Happy, and Peaceful Life...!

Regards
Robert Hurst

Chapter 6: Artificial Intelligence

The human race is the most intelligent species on Earth. Humans invented the computer, which was followed by a series of inventions that utterly transformed our way of life. While our reliance on technological devices increased exponentially, our methods of completing duties also evolved and became more sophisticated. AI is a branch of computer science designed to mimic the intelligence of the human mind. Machine learning (ML) is another important AI-related term.

AI enables computers and associated devices to solve problems and make swift decisions in the manner of the human mind. AI has been defined in a variety of ways over time, but in its simplest form, it is a combination of computer science and data that can activate problem-solving techniques. ML is an essential component of the system. The combination of machine learning and data enables AI to produce the finest results.

However, it is essential to comprehend the purpose of AI. People may believe it is a replacement for humans, but its purpose is to augment human contributions and abilities. This perspective renders AI a valuable asset for society and the business sector in particular.

The obvious query that arises is whether or not a device or machine can think like the human mind.

The beauty of the human intellect is its capacity for thought and rationality. AI was developed to provide machines with a sense of reasoning similar to that of the human intellect. Therefore, systems are designed and built to exhibit human-like behavior, advice, and explanations to users. Mankind designs and develops machines to reason and act like humans.

AI is unquestionably a science that has evolved from disciplines such as computer science, psychology, mathematics, biology, engineering, and linguistics. In addition, it includes functions that can readily identify and operate as a human mind to reason, learn, and advise users.

Now, another question arises: how are AI-assisted systems distinct from conventional systems?

Without AI, a computer program will only respond to the specific query posed by the user. However, a system powered by AI is also able to provide generic responses.

If modifications are made to a program without AI, the system's structure may endure significant alterations. In contrast, a program with AI will not exhibit any changes in its structure, even after minute modifications or the addition of information.

A significant difference between these programs is that a program without AI will not readily accept changes, whereas a program with AI will accept changes without affecting the program's fundamental structure.

AI component parts

A smartphone or smartwatch that is commonly used by people is designed and aided by artificial intelligence. Large and small manufacturing divisions, various types of voice assistants, and robots—artificial intelligence is everywhere. Companies rely on AI to enhance their consumer interactions in order to increase sales. A classic illustration of this theory is the use of chatbots by customer-centric websites to assist customers and respond to their questions in order to maximize customer satisfaction. Consequently, AI's dominance can be observed and observed almost everywhere in the business industry, and the primary benefit that companies derive from AI is their ability to automate functions.

If all of these interests you, then you should attempt to comprehend how AI works. Various factors contribute to the success of AI's operations and its operation. What are the AI's components?

Learning

Both humans and machines can make errors. Humans are constantly learning, and machines have been designed with a similar pattern but a distinct strategy. The AI learning process is based on trial and error. The problem-solving process continues until the optimal solution is found. The program is designed to store all moves in its database so that, the next time the same problem arises, it can use the correct orientation and provide solutions immediately. The AI learning quotient includes memorizing problem solutions, acquiring foreign languages and vocabulary, etc.

Similarly to how a human mind learns from its mistakes and attempts to avoid repeating them, AI-enabled computer programs have a problem-solving technique that includes thinking with available data input and using it to solve problems with minimal difficulty and error.

There are three distinct AI learning techniques: supervised, unsupervised, and semi-supervised.

Supervised Education

This is the type and extent of machine learning in artificial intelligence. It assists in training algorithms to generate output data with no or very few errors using input data. In this context, data is referred to as 'labeled' because it aides in producing the desired output. For instance, a teacher attempts to and assists students in achieving the correct answers to questions after learning a specific lesson. Similar to the unlabeled dataset, the labeled dataset aims to develop an algorithm that returns correct answers.

In supervised learning, the desired outcomes are accomplished because the trained datasets include input and output data, making the model accurate and efficient. The algorithm is designed to accurately adjust and reformat errors until sufficient precision is attained. Typically, classification and regression are the two categories of outcomes.

The accurate classification of data is made possible by algorithms. Using supervised learning, it is possible to solve a large number of real-world problems, for instance. In emails, the separation of the spam folder from the inbox folder is a classic example. Classifying customer feedback as positive or negative is another common classification example. Linear classifiers, random forests, support vector machines, k-nearest neighbor, and decision trees are popular classification algorithms.

Regression is useful for comprehending quantitative independent and dependent variables. Logistic, linear, and polynomial regression are prominent algorithms in regression. It can be used to derive sales reports for enterprises. Using postal codes to predict real estate prices is another useful example.

Supervised learning is utilized in audio, image, handwriting, bioinformatics, and email spam detection. Pattern recognition is yet another application of supervised learning. This enables architectural and construction firms to implement cost-effective measures for the construction of smart complexes, factories, and infrastructure.

Unsupervised Instruction

Unsupervised learning employs unlabeled data, whereas supervised learning employs labeled data. So, in this case, the algorithm seeks similarities in data to identify unexpected occurrences. This format is prevalent in association and clustering applications. Unsupervised learning can independently classify and aggregate data, unlike supervised learning, which requires labeled data. Unsupervised learning is unquestionably used to treat more complex problems than supervised learning, but the results are also highly ambiguous.

Semi-Supervised Education

This lies between supervised and unsupervised learning, as the name suggests. It is applicable to partially labeled data. It is excellent for situations requiring supervised learning, but due to a lack of labeled data, semi-supervised learning becomes the obvious option. It uses labeled data to designate unlabeled data, and work will continue until all data is sorted and trained according to the newly acquired labels. In facial recognition, for instance, distinct images of people are clustered by similarity in order to identify a picture by labeling a clustered image.

Reasoning

The most fascinating aspect of artificial intelligence is its ability to reason like a human intellect. Different approaches and deductions may apply to a given circumstance; therefore, reasoning enables the application of intellect to solve the problem. The two types of inferences are inductive and deductive. Consideration of the inferential case guarantees the solution's conclusion. In the case of inductive reasoning, however, failure results in an accident. Successful deductive inferences are computed by computer programs. Rational thought entails resonating and arriving at solutions by drawing pertinent inferences.

A Professional Guide to Affiliate Marketing

Obviously, this information will be included in the newsletters. Among the most essential information that has already been written.

There is still time for the marketer to compose recommendations for those who seek credible sources for the promoted products. There is also time to post comments on how to become a successful affiliate marketer on a website filled with wannabes.

Two objectives accomplished simultaneously. The marketer may advertise both the product and the program in which they participate. Who knows, perhaps someone will decide to join.

Time passes quickly. Missed lunch but is satisfied with the completed duties. Bedtime....

Okay, this may not be completed in a single day. However, this gives you an indication of how a dedicated affiliate marketer spends their marketing day.

What's up with that triumph looming in the distance?

What Online Affiliate Marketers Need to Survive

Currently, every affiliate marketer seeks a lucrative market that provides the highest profits. Occasionally, I believe that a magical formula makes them readily accessible. Actually, the situation is more complicated. This is a marketing best practice that has been demonstrated through years of effort and commitment. There are internet marketing strategies that have worked in the past and continue to work in the affiliate marketing industry today. These three marketing best practices will help you increase sales and thrive in network marketing. What are these strategies?

Each product you sell should have its own web page. Do not combine everything to save money on web hosting. It is beneficial to have a website dedicated to every product. Always include product evaluations on your website to provide visitors with an overview of the benefits your product offers. Additionally, include user reviews of the product. Ensure that you are prepared to permit these customers to use your name and image on the website of the product you are selling.

You can also write articles highlighting the use of your products and add them to your website as additional pages. Make your page appealing and include a call to exchange information. Every headline should encourage readers to continue reading and make contact. Note your distinctive characteristics. This helps readers understand and be interested in the page's content. We offer a complimentary report to our readers.

If at all possible, place it at the top of the page so that it cannot be missed. Create an autoresponder that sends email to individuals who input their information in the signup box. According to research, sales are typically concluded after the seventh contact with a potential client. Only two things can occur on a website. Closed sales or prospects who never return after leaving the page. Putting valuable information in their inbox at one point can help them remember the product they were considering purchasing and let them know when the sale has ended. Ensure that your content focuses on a specific purpose for purchasing a product. Avoid sounding like a sales proposal. Focus on key aspects such as how your product makes life easier and more enjoyable. Include an engaging subject in your correspondence. Avoid using the word "free" whenever feasible. Because antiquated spam filters eliminate such content before anyone can read it. Convince the recipients of your free report that they are missing out by not using your products and services. Bring customers to your products.

If your website's visitors are uninterested in the products you have to offer, you are likely one of these one-time visitors. Write magazine and electronic report articles. This allows you to discover posts that are directed toward your target audience, which may be of interest to you. Write at least two articles of 300-600 words per week. By continually composing and updating these articles, you can attract hundreds of your target audience to your website every day.

Keep in mind that only 1 in 100 individuals are likely to purchase your product or utilize your service. When thoroughly considered, the above strategy is not difficult to implement. This requires both work and a strategy. Consider these suggestions for various affiliate marketing programs. It is not possible for every marketer to maintain and prosper in this industry. Plus, consider the enormous salary you'll receive!

How to Become a Niche Market Super Affiliate

In recent years, web hosting has expanded more than ever before. Demand for web hosting is at an all-time high as an increasing number of businesses enter the market and recognize its many advantages. It appears to be a current trend.

Alone in 2005, 38 million individuals created their first website. Remember that the majority of these sites offer multiple affiliate programs from which individuals can choose and sign up.

It only has one meaning. Now it is simpler to locate the ideal web host for your application. Expect opportunities from web hosting companies of superior quality that stand out from the competition. Then the one who suffers is the incompetent, not the expert.

Customer service is a primary consideration when selecting a web host. It is becoming evident that conventional advertising has lost its effectiveness. Many individuals favor selecting a web host based on what they see and hear. In addition, it is based on the recommendations of those who have attempted and succeeded.

This is an exceptional opportunity for web hosting partners and resellers alike. Finding the appropriate web hosting and software is no longer a challenge, as there are hundreds available.

How to use web hosting to become a successful affiliate in your niche. Everyone who requires a website requires a web hosting company to host their website. There is currently no industry leader in hosting, so many individuals choose their providers based on recommendations. I typically receive them from individuals who have utilized web hosting services.

With so many providers offering affiliate programs, affiliates typically choose the one that best suits them. Consider the product that you are promoting. Allow them to shape your website and ensure that their interests align with yours. If you've been with the same host for a while and haven't seen much progress despite your best efforts, you should look for a new host. You are not required to have one in order to join one. You were at your lowest point, after which things will improve.

Try it out. Check to see if your web host has an affiliate program that you can join if you are extremely satisfied with their services. Rather than pay, why not do the opposite? they compensate you Simply posting a tiny "offer" or "hosted" link at the bottom of the page is sufficient to establish a partnership.

Why spend money on web hosting if you do not require it? Get paid for positive reviews of your web host.

Always remember to select a web host with a stellar reputation for customer service. There are also numerous affiliate hosting programs. The remaining affiliate programs will also be posted. It is a program that pays a specified monthly percentage for referred consumers. This enables you to secure a stable income source. Indeed, perseverance can result in substantial accomplishment in this field.

There are numerous niches waiting for the right companion to help them realize and accomplish their goals. Knowing where to begin instills sufficient confidence in your abilities and the positive outcomes you will achieve.

Web hosting is an affiliate market in which you can attempt to earn a sustainable income. Remember that business success requires time, effort, and persistence.

No one has yet created the ideal affiliate market. However, some individuals understand how to succeed in such a market. Knowing the type of market you are in and taking advantage of it is all that is required.

Numerous associate programs! Which option do you select? Ask inquiries prior to enrolling in an affiliate program. Conduct research on the program options you intend to pursue.

Get some answers. Because it will determine your success in the future. Is there a participation fee? The majority of affiliate programs offered today are gratis. Why are you okay with individuals charging a small fee prior to registration?

When are payments for taxes issued? Each curriculum is unique. Others are monthly, quarterly, etc. Select your preferable payment schedule. Most affiliate programs have a minimum fee threshold that must be met or exceeded before payments can be issued. What is your sales success rate? The average number of clicks required for a banner or text link to generate sales, taking into account all affiliate metrics. This factor is crucial because it indicates how much traffic you must generate to earn your sales commission.

How are affiliate site referrals monitored, and for how long are they stored? To track referrals, you must have faith in your program. This is the only method of crediting purchases. How long these individuals remain in the system is also crucial. This is because some visitors may not make a purchase on their initial visit, but may return in the future. Determine whether you can still receive credit for sales made months after a particular date.

What kinds of affiliate statistics are offered? Choose an affiliate program that provides comprehensive statistics. When you decide to review them, you should be able to access them online. It is always up to you to affirm

Understanding how many impressions, views, and sales your website has generated is essential. Impressions are the number of times a website visitor viewed a banner or text link. People who click on a banner or text link are considered views.

In addition to sales commissions, do affiliate programs pay for impressions and views? Additionally, impressions and views contribute to sales commission income, so it is essential to generate revenue. This is especially crucial if the program you're utilizing offers a low rate of return to satisfy this rate. Who is the internet retailer? You must know who you are doing business with to ensure that you are a trustworthy organization. They are familiar with the products they sell and the average production volume. The more you know about the affiliate program providers, the simpler it will be for you to determine if the program is a good fit for your website. Is the affiliate program multilevel or singlelevel? Programs with tiers only pay for the commerce you generate. A two-tier program pays both the company and the affiliates who are sponsored by the company. Some affiliate programs offer a modest commission for each new affiliate that you recruit. including rent.

What is the total cost? Many programs charge a fee ranging from 20% to 80% (in some instances 100%!).0.01% to 0.05% is the cost per access. If you discover a program that also pays for impressions, you will not be compensated very well. As the statistics indicate, it is now clear why average sales volume and price are crucial.

Here are a few queries you should ask prior to enrolling in an affiliate program. Before implementing your selected program on your website, you should familiarize yourself with its essential features. Consider the following inquiries when selecting an affiliate program. This will assist you in selecting the appropriate program for your website from the many available options.

Chapter 7: Tracking And Optimization

A cunning SEO strategy for affiliate marketing resolves the traffic issue. You consistently attract visitors to your affiliate website. The only challenge would be converting the traffic into purchases.

Wouldn't that be incredible?
SEO stands for "search engine optimization" and refers to the optimization of online content for natural search engine results.

What then is affiliate marketing? When consumers seek online for products related to what you sell, SEO enhances the visibility of affiliate pages.

Traffic origins
Although your website may receive traffic from initiatives such as banner

ads or paid search, direct, referral, and search traffic are the three primary sources of website traffic. Consider tallying the number of visitors from each traffic source and the number of objectives attained by each source.

Monitoring and enhancing traffic sources

You'll need a Google Analytics account and to navigate to Acquisition » Channels to monitor your website's traffic sources. There, you can review your traffic sources and learn more about each one.

Monitoring instruments

Ahrefs is one of the SEO tools that is frequently recommended online. In terms of scale, it is second only to Google among website crawlers. The Ahrefs Site Audit function is the most effective SEO analysis instrument on the market, and SEO specialists cannot get enough of it. The tool identifies areas of your website that need to be enhanced for a higher search engine ranking. You will use

Ahrefs to identify your competitor's backlinks in order to use them as a starting point for your brand. This SEO tool can examine your website for broken links, provide an overview of your top-performing pages, and identify the most shared content in your niche.

Google Search Console is a free service that enables website owners to monitor and report on their website's visibility in Google search results. To submit your sitemap for indexing, all you need to do is authenticate your website by adding a code or utilizing Google Analytics. You do not need a Search Console account to appear in Google's search results, but you can use this account to manage what is highlighted and how your website is displayed. Using Search Console as an SEO analyzer, you can optimize your website for improved performance in Google search results and gain insight into how Google and its users perceive websites. The ability to submit web pages for indexing by search engines is especially beneficial for new websites.

The SEO community prefers marketing SEO tools such as SEMRush. Experts venerate them because they make it easy to evaluate your rankings, detect changes, and identify new ranking opportunities. The Domain vs. Domain study, which allows you to compare your website to those of your competitors, is one of the most popular features of this SEO tool. If you're searching for analytics reports to gain a deeper understanding of your website's traffic, search statistics, and competitors, you can compare keywords and domains. Using the On-Page SEO Checker, you can easily monitor your rankings and receive recommendations for improving your website's functionality.

Email Marketing

Even though much has been said and written about email marketing, it remains one of the most effective methods for promoting your products. If you want to implement a powerful strategy for member marketing without a website, you cannot simply ignore email marketing.

You can compile a list of email addresses manually or import them into a database and then create a targeted email marketing campaign. Add branching connections to the center, and you're all set. If you want to construct your own email list, you can search for retailers that provide sign-up assistance.

To convince someone to join, you will persuade them. Admission to a digital book, a free aid, or a free course is intelligent and will increase enrollment rates.

Physical Products and Administrations for Sale

While selling eBooks through platforms like JVZoo is a wonderful way to ensure that you retain the most profit, it also has its limitations. Despite what a few various advertisers may tell you, the most popular type of product sold online is still the actual variety.

Furthermore, this appears to be legitimate when viewed objectively. What is the approximate number of individuals who purchase genuine products? Almost everybody, correct? However, how many people do you believe might purchase an e-book at this time? Your Grandmother could not (unless via Kindle) because she has no notion how to utilize a PDF document. Likewise, your friend who could live without reading probably wouldn't anyway! Furthermore, this leaves you with a substantially smaller share of the market. As a subsidiary advertiser, how would we approach selling physical goods? The most popular option is to become an Amazon Associate.

Amazon's partner conspire is their version of a subsidiary program, and it is a highly alluring option for certain advertisers. If you conduct research on associate marketing, you'll most likely discover the following. Find that the vast majority of it focuses on selling digital products via JVZoo, ClickBank, and Commission Junction. On Amazon, the circumstance are unique. Amazon is currently sharing the profits with the manufacturer; however, they must pay for storage, transportation, and postage, so they cannot offer more than 4% or 8% at most. This means you will need to sell significantly more items at significantly higher prices in order to generate a profit. However, does this imply that you should terminate Amazon Associates? Not only is the sale of physical goods substantially more profitable than the sale of digital goods, but it is also significantly more profitable by a significant margin. Consider: Are you more likely to spend a lot of money on something you can hold and demonstrate to your companions, or something you must read on a computer screen? Even better, Amazon is a recognized brand and a trusted organization. This means they are significantly more likely to purchase with a single click!

Amazon has a vast catalog of items you can sell, ensuring that there is a suitable complement for virtually every article. else And finally, if someone clicks on your URL and ultimately makes a purchase on Amazon, you are compensated! If someone managed to purchase a second PC and you were to receive 8% of the purchase price, this could result in a substantial number of sold units. Regardless of whether you promote the product directly, as long as you send the customer to Amazon, you will receive the commission. What is the greatest action to take? Utilize both types of member marketing! However, do not avoid Amazon in light of the situation, or you will miss a significant opportunity! In later sections, you will learn how to advance Amazon items in a somewhat unanticipated manner to maximize their utility. (Note: One limitation of Amazon Associates is that you cannot earn money if you do not reside in a similar country. If you are located in the United Kingdom, you should ultimately direct your customers to Amazon UK. You can still make purchases through Amazon.com, but you will only be able to collect vouchers in exchange.)

Chapter 8: Various Methods For Selling Physical Goods

Amazon is undoubtedly not the most significant entity in the world when it comes to the sale of actual goods. There are innumerable physical stores and numerous manufacturers that offer member programs directly to advertisers. It could be argued that if you make the effort to search for other products, you can discover something that is much more directly relevant to your site's topic (and therefore more likely to sell). To locate these subsidiary initiatives, try searching Google with "member program" and the name of your field. Additionally, you can discover numerous records online for the best subsidiary projects in each industry. Another option is to coordinate with a manufacturer or dealer who does not provide a subsidiary program... after which you should inquire whether they would contemplate making one for you. If you figure out how to do this effectively, you can negotiate an exclusive agreement and potentially earn a substantial commission. Clearly, for everything to fall into place, you should have the option to demonstrate that you have the scope and impact to make their time and effort worthwhile.

Providing Services

Another option is to try selling assistance or SAS (Software as a Service). This option is perhaps the most advantageous! The rationale for this is that numerous administrations offer recurring commissions. Suppose you are able to convince someone to join a wagering website. Some wagering websites will pay a commission on a customer's lifetime earnings with the brand. Likewise, if you can persuade somebody to join a facilitating account, or if nothing else to join a common support, you will frequently discover that you are.

7. DISTRIBUTE DISCOUNT CODES.

Share promotional codes

Frequently, merchants compose a list of online marketing materials for affiliates to use as part of their affiliate program. Banner graphics and email marketing content typically make the shortlist. However, it doesn't harm to ask your affiliate partners if they have active, redeemable discount codes for the products you're promoting.

In addition to converting people who haven't tried the products you're recommending yet, these coupon codes do an excellent job of converting those who haven't tried them yet. Approximately 89% of millennial consumers will test a new brand in exchange for a discount.

Once you have a discount code to distribute to your audience, you can do so by:

Sharing it with direct affiliate links to purchase on social media.

Sending an email that directs your audience towards the sale.

modifying affiliate-related website content to include the promotional code Including "discount" in the meta description of your review pages will entice users to click-through.

Sprocker Lovers, for instance, published a product review that appears on the first page of results for "Bella and Duke review." As an incentive for users to click through and shop via the affiliate link, the meta title plainly indicates the availability of a discount code.

8:POST PRODUCT ROUND UP.

Post product aggregations

How do you determine whether the product you're writing about is worth your time? There is a possibility that your product review will fail, generating few affiliate sales and leaving you wishing you had focused on a different product.

"One of the biggest mistakes I've seen new affiliate marketers make is writing lengthy, in-depth product reviews for products that simply do not convert," says Affiliate founder Monica Lent.The end result is a tremendous amount of effort with little to show for it.

"Rather, affiliates should reverse the sequence in which they produce content. Create product roundups (e.g., "best camera for travel") to determine which products are most popular with your audience.

"Once you've determined which products are converting, separate them into individual reviews and link to them internally as supplementary content," Monica advises. "Not only does this strategy help you create affiliate content more efficiently, but it's also great for SEO."

Here is a wonderful illustration of this in practice. This Is Why I'm Broke publishes gift guides for nearly every possible recipient, including parents, coworkers, and sister-in-laws. The publisher receives a commission for each transaction of a recommended item from the gift guide.

Write a product evaluation and tutorial.

Write product evaluations and how-to guides

Did you know that almost nine out of ten consumers consult product reviews prior to making a purchase? By composing search engine-optimized reviews for affiliate products, you will reach individuals who have already begun the purchasing process.

Consider the following scenario: you are publishing a review of Allbirds' running shoes. You have included the keyphrase "Allbirds shoes review", which is searched by 1,500 persons per month.

If you have people click your affiliate link, you will earn a commission on the transaction, even if they were already interested in purchasing the product prior to discovering your site.

REPORT ON AFFILIATE LINK DISCUSSIONS.

Report conversions from affiliate link clicks

How do you know your affiliate marketing strategy's products are selling?

As with any digital marketing campaign, you should schedule regular reminders to review your most crucial metrics, such as:

Clicks. A low number of clicks on a heavily promoted product may indicate that your audience is uninterested in the item you are promoting.

Ratio of successful conversions. The proportion of individuals who clicked on your affiliate link and made a purchase. More height is preferable.

Earned a living. The quantity of money earned through the promotion of a product. The majority of this information can be found in Google Analytics. Affiliate networks and partners will also have access to an interface displaying this data.

The purpose of reporting is to identify the most popular and profitable products so that you can continue promoting them and deprioritize those that aren't selling.

Find your most popular product and request a commission increase from the manufacturer. Clearly demonstrate your value as an affiliate. Promise to continue doing excellent work and generate more revenue if they can provide your audience with a highly exclusive discount code.

Affiliate marketing, also known as offshoot or subsidiary advertising (showcasing). Member marketing is a cycle in which distributors earn a commission by promoting a product or service created by another retailer or promoter. The member partner is compensated for delivering a specific result to the retailer or promoter.

In addition, subsidiary marketing is a form of advertising in which a company pays third-party distributors to generate traffic or promote its products and services. External distributors are members, and the commission expense encourages them to seek out opportunities to advance the organization.

Typically, the result is an agreement. However, some initiatives may compensate you for leads, free-trial clients, website visits, or application downloads.

Partner programs are typically open to participation, so you do not need to worry about excessive startup costs. This presentation-based opportunity can help you transition from a part-time job to a profitable web-based business by allowing you to earn a decent wage.

Affiliate marketing models.

Taking a look at some of the companies that engage in affiliate marketing will provide you with motivation and evidence that this is a legitimate and lucrative income stream.

The models of affiliate programs are as follows: Amazon

Amazon Partners, Amazon's affiliate marketing program, is one of the most well-known models. Amazon Partners currently holds the largest share of the industry's member organizations (45.81%), followed by CJ Subsidiary (8.14%) and Rakuten Subsidiary Organization (7.85%).

Amazon Offshoots offers a variety of products from a vast array of categories. It is an exceptional method for novices to enter ancillary promotion. Creators, distributors, and influencers can use Amazon member connections to direct their audience to product recommendations. From the connection reference, you can bring funds for purchases that qualify.Amazon Partners, its subsidiary promotion program, is one of the world's largest member subsidiary advertising programs.

Designers, distributors, and influencers sign up to share Amazon products and services on their websites or applications, and are subsequently compensated for the sales their sites generate.

Amazon imposes stringent requirements on the websites and applications that host its advertisements. For instance, destinations should not reuse content from other sites or designers and should be accessible to the general public. According to all accounts, sites should be dynamic, with new pleasure and appropriateness. For instance, they should not contain repulsive or hostile substances, promote violence or illegal demonstrations, or contain any content deemed to be offensive to others.

Endorsement is contingent on a thorough review by Amazon staff and the achievement of a certified transaction share (three within 180 days of the application). In the event that a submission is rejected, it will not be eligible for reevaluation. Once approved, commissions are earned when site visitors purchase products or services from Amazon.

Amazon Partners can earn up to 20% in commissions on eligible transactions. Fixed rates are based on item and program classifications. Amazon offers distinct commissions on specific occasions as an added bonus.

Consider Sprocker Sweethearts as an example. Website owner Elise Dopson authored a blog post titled "Are Spaniels Good Running Companions? and Six Safety Tips for Running." In the article, she suggests that spaniels should don a high-visibility dog coat while out jogging at night.

Execution of the Sprocker Sweethearts web page subsidiary initiative

If a user needs to purchase a high-visibility dog garment, they can click the link and proceed to Amazon to complete the transaction.

The Shopify e-commerce platform

The Shopify Partner Program is an organization of business visionaries, educators, formidable forces, and creators who send Shopify recommendations. It is permitted to pursue the program; the only requirement is to apply.

Once approved, partners receive a unique external reference to share with their audience. They are compensated when someone joins through their referral link.

Shopify Offshoots typically earn $58 for each referral who subscribes to a paid Shopify plan. Offshoots can acquire as much or as little as they need, with the amount largely dependent on how much time they devote to their subsidiary marketing strategy.

Physically fit

Water bottle retailers Healthiest used partners' advertising to build a one million dollar brand. Instead of taking the conventional member route, it utilized Instagram influencers to promote the launch of its flagship product, the WB-1 bottle.
The brand continues to work with powerhouse accounts, including those with 100,000 or more followers. It collaborates with approximately 300 creators per month to create content for business sectors and sells the product on a large scale.

Electrical Wire Cutter

Wirecutter, a 2016 acquisition of The New York Times affiliate site promoting products and devices, states that it only makes recommendations after "overwhelming revealing, talking, and testing by groups of veteran writers, researchers, and specialists."

- BuzzFeed

BuzzFeed's shopping section began as a gift guide and expanded to include surveys of various product categories.
The website is novel in that it covers a variety of common topics and provides best picks at three different price points. BuzzFeed's product reviews are extremely comprehensive, which provides a great deal of value to the reader. As specific examples, we offer a blog post on tissue and another on white blouses for women.

- Urikar

According to ShareASale data, retailer Urikar offers a high-ticket member program with average commissions of $1,460. It distributes health and wellness products such as back massage tools, indoor and outdoor exercise equipment, and accessories.

Urikar offers a 10% commission on all sales, which can add up quickly if you have a large following and are a wellness influencer. Its most popular product, a computer based intelligence controlled muscle massager, retails for $139.99, so you will earn $13.99 per sale. In addition, Urikar's program provides a dedicated record manager and interface for monitoring changes and transactions.

- Etsy

Etsy (ETSY), a global online marketplace for uncommon items and other unusual items, promotes its products through various channels, including member promoting partners. To apply, candidates must submit an online application via the subsidiary program's gateway. To qualify as an Etsy affiliate marketing partner, applicants must be at least 18 years old, have a functional, exceptional website, have a brand identity, and meet other requirements.

When an item is endorsed, Etsy pays a commission to the partner for any sales they generate as a result of their site's promotion of the item. Commission rates vary and are reflected in the quote price. Etsy sellers can become members, but they cannot earn commissions on their products without special permission. Etsy asserts that it may terminate an agreement at any time and for any reason, and that it may continue making payments for any valid reason.

- eBay

eBay's Partner Organization is eBay's member advertising program that compensates partners for promoting their own listings outside of eBay Inc. (EBAY). The partner receives a commission and may receive a credit against their final merchant fees.

eBay partners can also earn commissions on the items of other sellers.

Commissions are earned when a buyer bids on or purchases an item within 24 hours of clicking the eBay buy link on the member's website. For submitted bids, the commission is paid if the purchaser wins the transaction within approximately 10 days of the bid.

The commission rates vary from 1% to 4% based on the classification of the sold items. Approximately $550 will be paid for each successful transaction. Due to their low income streams, gift certificates, items sold by charitable organizations, and exceptional advancements are typically disqualified as qualifying bargains.

Chapter 9: How To Address The Drop Shipping Issue

If you're Drop shipping and haven't yet made any money, don't worry because there's nothing you can do about it if, for example, you're Drop shipping with AliExpress.

There are alternatives to AliExpress that will help you create a superior shopping experience for your customers than AliExpress!

And that should suffice, right?

If you are making a profit on a product, you may want to acquire it in bulk and handle the remainder yourself.

You could also utilize a fulfillment center like Amazon FBA.

Thus, you have complete control over the box's appearance and may include any accessories you see fit. You also benefit from faster shipping periods compared to dropshipping from China.

You also do not have to fret about clients ordering multiple items and requiring multiple packages to be sent.

It is not always possible to submit multiple-item orders.

This occurs most frequently when using AliExpress for Drop shipping, but it is also possible when using another platform that connects you with multiple Drop shipping suppliers.

If a customer places an order for multiple products and you use different Drop shipping suppliers for each of those products, you will not be able to dispatch those products to the customer in a single shipment.

This means that your customers may receive multiple packages and may assert that their order is incomplete after receiving the initial shipment.

In addition, you will incur multiple shipping costs.

Each distinct shipment that must be sent to a customer incurs additional shipping fees!

How to address the Drop shipping issue

Select fewer AliExpress suppliers, for instance, to increase the likelihood that your customer's order will arrive in a single cargo.

You may also include a related query on your Frequently Asked Questions page.

Don't overlook providing superior customer service.

There may be concerns about quality control.

You engage in Drop shipment. The item will never be viewed.

If you never see the product, you may not become aware of quality issues until it is too late.

Perhaps one day you will receive a deluge of emails from unhappy customers about your products.

How to address the Drop shipping issue

If this is a concern, you should always request a sample from the Dropshipping supplier.

A sample is essentially ordering the goods yourself and having them delivered to your residence in order to evaluate the delivery time, packaging, and quality of the product.

This allows you to evaluate the product's quality for yourself. Using the sample product, you can also create your own product images and recordings!

Inventory deficits

As stated previously, drop shipping provides little influence over a variety of variables.

The same holds true for the inventory of your Drop shipping provider.

It is possible that your products will sell exceptionally well, and that your Drop shipping provider will be unable to keep up with demand.

Thankfully, this one is easy to repair!

How to address the Drop shipping issue

Communicate with your Drop shipping provider and ask how much inventory they have and how rapidly they can obtain more.

In the event that the provider of your Drop shipping service actually runs out of stock, you will be able to rapidly switch to a different Drop shipping provider that carries the same products.

This is straightforward to do on AliExpress; simply search the product and you will likely find 10 to 20 other AliExpress sellers selling the same or a slightly modified version of the product.

You may even be able to resolve this issue before your Drop-shipping provider runs out.

Simply send a message to some Drop shipping suppliers and ask them the same questions you asked your current supplier.

You may also acquire samples from these suppliers to ensure that if your current Drop shipping provider runs out of stock, you will still be able to fulfill orders with high-quality goods!

Lower earnings

Because Drop shipping does not offer volume discounts, it has a hidden "cost."

Instead of paying less for a large inventory, you will almost undoubtedly spend more per item sold, resulting in a smaller profit.

In contrast to conventional wholesalers, who sell in bulk, a Drop shipping supplier sells you a single product for each order you place.

As a result, they must endure the costs associated with storing and insuring the products, as well as staffing and packaging individual items.

Wholesalers already have very low profit margins and rely heavily on high-volume purchases to generate a profit;

therefore, when these additional costs are factored in, the wholesaler is compelled to increase the price of individual items.

Consequently, your profit margins will decrease because you will be paying your Drop shipping provider more.

How to address the Drop shipping issue

One solution would be to increase product sales.

This may seem apparent, but I thought it was worth mentioning!

For example, selling 10 items for a $10 profit yields $100, while selling 100 items for the same price yields $1000.

As a result, you will be inundated with work and run the risk of orders not being fulfilled as expected.

For this reason, some individuals favor high-priced Drop shipping items over cheaper ones.

You must understand from the outset that although you may pay more to the supplier, you will not incur additional costs such as warehousing the products and shipping them to all of your customers.

Your supplier handles all of these particulars. Therefore, it is essential that you choose the appropriate AliExpress suppliers (or something other than AliExpress) from the beginning of your Drop shipping journey.

Nonetheless, if you observe consistent sales of one or more products, it would be prudent to import them in quantities from a website such as Alibaba.

Keep in mind that even if your cost per unit is lower because you purchase in bulk and your supplier does not ship the products to your customers, you will incur additional expenses.

It is essential to realize that although importing it in volume and distributing it to your customers requires more effort, it is less expensive (or you can use a fulfillment service). It will certainly be beneficial.

Consider how much additional effort you can invest in the entire delivery and packaging:

You can guarantee delivery within one to three business days as opposed to one to three weeks.

Include a business card or discount coupon for a second purchase in the gift!

For example, Packhelp can be used to brand your shipment.

Refunds can be challenging.

Choosing reputable Drop shipping suppliers will reduce the likelihood of this occurring, but it is still possible.

It could take up to two to three weeks for the product(s) to arrive at your customer's location if you are drop shipping from China.

This, coupled with the fact that you will have no control over the quality of the product, increases the likelihood of refund requests.

How to address the Drop shipping issue

The simplest way to manage refunds and returns when Drop shipping is to determine whether it is more cost-effective to allow customers to keep the product and ship a replacement.

If not, have the consumer return the item to the supplier.

You must only decide whether to pay the return fees or not.

Customer service can be difficult.

As previously stated, you have no control over the supply chain.

You will not readily be able to resolve a customer complaint.

If you are unable to answer a customer's query, you must first consult with your Drop shipping provider, which may take time.

How to address the Drop shipping issue

To be as concise as possible:

Provide outstanding client service!

Customer service is crucial for retaining clients in your Drop shipping store.

It will even reduce the number of refund requests you receive.

Always endeavor to be as kind and understanding as possible when responding to a customer's questions or requests.

Numerous other opponents

Most Drop-shipping companies falter due to a lack of originality.

Numerous individuals are currently learning about Drop shipping and launching Drop shipping stores.

For example, enter "Drop shipping" into Google Trends.

Since so many of these "gurus" promoted it as an easy way to make money online, everyone wants a piece.

But what is the most tragic thing?

The majority do nothing to enhance their Drop shipping store.

They launch their company, import certain products without modification, and commence advertising.

This indicates that many Drop shippers are selling identical products with identical descriptions, potentially from the same Drop shipping suppliers.

Having the same product is not necessarily a negative thing, but having the same images, descriptions, and so on is useless!

How to address the Drop shipping issue

Therefore, what can be done about the issue of excessive competition?

Simple. Attempt to best them!

Do not attempt to save time by duplicating everything.

Because you're establishing a legitimate business with your Drop shipping store, exert effort.

Affiliate marketing refers to initiatives designed to increase a company's product sales by establishing partnerships with affiliates or publishers, who are independent online sales representatives. In contrast to conventional contextual advertising, affiliate marketing systems facilitate direct communication between content creators and advertisers.

Effective affiliate marketing campaigns may generate more revenue for publishers than contextual advertising platforms such as Google AdSense. Affiliate marketing is a fruitful method of product promotion from the advertiser's perspective due to the compensation structure's dependence on the publisher's output. Only if the publisher successfully facilitates a sale is the advertiser required to pay.

Affiliate marketing organizations

Important parties involved in affiliate marketing transactions include the following:

- Product Merchant - A product merchant is the proprietor of the product that must be advertised; they are also known as the product creator or product owner.
- Affiliate Network Platform - This is a platform that provides promotional tools, resources, and links. Affiliate Network acts as an intermediary between the Affiliate Marketer and the Product Merchant.
- Affiliate Merchant - This is a company that focuses on marketing and generating traffic to brands through a network of affiliate websites. As a result, they create a variety of advertisements, including text links, static banners, flash banners, video ads, and sometimes a combination of several of these, for placement on affiliate websites. Affiliate merchants utilize Affiliate network platforms for this purpose.
- Affiliate Marketer (Affiliate/Publisher): This individual has a website that displays affiliate merchant links and advertisements. The affiliate marketer attempts to advertise

the product through content (such as articles, product reviews, how-to guides, and product comparisons).The majority of affiliate merchants have their own internal platform. However, affiliate merchants occasionally utilize an external Affiliate network platform. Consequently, it is common for the Affiliate Network Platform and the Affiliate Merchant to be treated similarly. Technically speaking, however, they are not identical.

In this book, the terms Affiliate Network Platform and Affiliate Merchant will be used interchangeably. In some instances, we will use the term "Affiliate Network Provider" to refer to a combination of the two. However, it should be emphasized that an Affiliate Merchant cannot operate without an Affiliate Network Platform. Therefore, whenever the phrase "affiliate merchant" is used, "affiliate network platform" is implied.

Affiliate Marketing's Mechanisms

The steps that follow illustrate how affiliate marketing functions:

- A vendor solicits the assistance of an affiliate network provider to promote his or her products.
- The network provider and affiliate merchant concur on the respective revenues of each party. Additionally, they strike an agreement on affiliate payments.
- The network provider develops a mechanism for autonomously generating product-specific connections (Affiliate ID) based on information from the affiliate marketer and the product merchant (such as the product name).
- The Affiliate Marketer contacts the Network Provider, registers, and is provided with automatically-generated links to post on his website or blog based on his registration credentials.
- The affiliate marketer utilizes the provided link to connect specific content or spaces.
- The Affiliate publishes content on the blog that piques the interest of readers. 7. The reader examines the information and, if persuaded to

purchase the advertised product, clicks the Affiliate link.

• Upon selecting the hyperlink, the reader (potential customer) is taken to the product page of the product merchant.

• If the consumer decides to purchase the product, the Affiliate's marketing efforts result in a successful sale. • Both the Affiliate Network and the product vendor maintain a record of the transaction details.After a successful sale, payment is credited to the Affiliate's account. The expiration date is determined by the security period. The majority of Affiliate networks offer shorter than 30-day security terms. The security period ensures that the Affiliate will not be compensated if the customer returns the item and requests a refund. The security period is determined by the return policy of the product merchant and the additional waiting time imposed by the Affiliate Network.

www.ingramcontent.com/pod-product-compliance
Lightning Source LLC
Chambersburg PA
CBHW050252120526
44590CB00016B/2317